HOW TO TURN YOUR
MESSAGE
OR EXPERTISE
INTO A
PROFITABLE
BEST-SELLING BOOK

By 4X's New York Time Bestseller

WAHIDA CLARK

Wahida Clark Distribution
60 Evergreen Place
Suite 904A
East Orange, New Jersey 07018
1-866-910-6920
www.wclarkdistribution.com
www.wclarkpublishing.com

Library of Congress Cataloging-In-Publication Data:
Wahida Clark
How To Turn Your Message, Cause or Expertise into a Best-
Selling Book
ISBN 13-digit 978-1-477325-2-0
ISBN 10-digit 97814773252

1. Writing- 2. Book Publishing 3. References- 4. Book
Distribution- 5. Coaching

Creative Direction & Layout by
Art Supplied Gfx
www.artdiggs.com

Printed in USA

MY MISSION

My mission should you choose to accept, is to make sure that in 45 days or less, you seize this moment to get that 1st draft of the outline or book you've been struggling to write, finish or get out of your head, so that the weight of accomplishment is off your shoulders, another big win is under your belt, and use your book to spread your message, establish yourself as the expert or get more speaking engagements or clients.

Foreword

By Four-Time New York Times Bestseller . . . WAHIDA CLARK!

No! Your Book doesn't have to be 300 pages! This is the answer to one of the most frequent questions that I am asked.

YOU are the Expert. You are trying to get YOUR Message across. You are focused on bringing awareness to YOUR Cause.

In today's social media, tell me what's in it for me, tell it to me fast, is what you are trying to tell me going to help solve my problem now, or at least point me in the right direction, climates . . . Long is wrong!

Get to the point. That's what this book does, and that is what this book will show you how to do.

This book is all about Turning your Message, Cause, Expertise, or your Business Card into a Book, just like this.

CONTENTS

INTRODUCTION

"You may not get rich off your book, but you can get rich because of it." – Wahida Clark

The book business has been good to me. The business of books has taken me on a journey that most authors only dream of. So, I know first-hand that having a book or being an author or expert/author can give you instant celebrity status. Because of my books I've rubbed elbows with platinum selling and Grammy award-winning artists, *New York Times* best-selling authors, actors, actresses, the top comedians, NFL, NBA, and MLB players, rappers, you name it . . . Yes, this has been my networking experience all because of being an author. I get called to do speaking engagements and get flown in to host book events and parties. I am asked to be a guest on talk, TV, and podcast shows.

Having a book opens doors you had no clue that you had a key to. And like I said, "You may not get rich off your book, but you can get rich because of it." My books have made it possible for me to receive six-figure advances, and now I am in negotiations for TV and movie deals. My books provide me with a monthly income, residual. Meaning, while I am asleep my books are selling.

A book can give you power. If you don't have one yet, continue reading . . .

How To Turn your Expertise into a Profitable, Bestselling Book . . . Like This is obviously the title of this book. But my first choice for the title and what this book is really about is, How To Turn Your Message, Cause, Expertise, or Your Business Card into a Book Just Like This!

But welcome to the 21st Century Social-Media-Era, in which all marketing has been taken to the latest stratosphere! There are so many ways to market a book: YouTube, Facebook, Instagram, Roku, Fire TV . . . the list goes on and on and on. And the fantastic thing is all of these marketing platforms include the oldest but time-tested trend where AUTHORS are considered the EXPERTS and the new money getting ROCK STARS!

I recall seeing Stacey Abrams on the campaign trail as she was running for Governor of Georgia. I thought, *she is an excellent speaker. She's smart and comes across as very warm and genuine.* I made a mental note that I would love to get to know her. However, I still came away only partly clear on what she actually stood for or what she believed. I wanted her to really sell me. And of course, that's when it hit me! If she had a book like this, she would have the time and space needed to lay out her message or outline her agenda, mission, and beliefs, so that she could reach her base or potential base. Ms. Abrams would then ignite! Those were my personal thoughts and opinion. And yes, you probably guessed it, she now has a book published. But when I first wrote this she didn't.

Whatever your message is, be it Mental Health, Politics, The Healing Effects of Cannabis, Human Trafficking, Women's Empowerment, Climate Change, Branding, Children and Video Games, you name it . . . They all can be easily put into a book just like this.

But not only will a book like this get your message across in great detail, it is simple to put together and it sets you up for future paid speaking engagements, your very own talk or TV show, more clients, and so much more.

If you were at a conference or event amongst your colleagues or peers, and the panelist introduced everyone, and you were the only one who had "author" added to your profile, who do you think the audience would gravitate toward? Who do you think the attendees would rather do business with?

Being an author gives you an edge over your competition, peers, and colleagues; and further propels you as the more knowledgeable expert in the eyes of your prospects.

A book just like this is the best business card you can have, the best salesman you can have, and by far the best spokesman you could have. Why? Nothing beats attending a conference or an event where everyone is handing out regular business cards, and you are handing out copies of your signed book with your regular business card tucked inside.

Remember:

An author is considered the expert. Customers and clients prefer to buy from experts over the non-expert or amateur. Your base prospects (audience) will understand or get your full message or cause if everything is laid out in a book. Below is a list of reasons your message in book format will reach your intended target:

Experts have experience.

Experts have credibility.

Experts have solutions.

Experts have authority.

Experts are leaders.

Experts have celebrity.

Experts create opportunity.

Rest assured your message will not be glossed over. What you stand for will be in black and white. What you are advocating for and why will be clearly spelled out.

Becoming an Author

Anyone can become an author as long as they have something to say that people would like to read, learn, or become aware of. Becoming an author doesn't have to be difficult. And why this is great for you is, I am a four-time *New York Times* Best Seller. My team and I can assist you every step of the way! With the help of my expert publishing and branding team, you will be well on your way to becoming an author in no time. And for you authors and experts who are ready to take it to the next level, with the help of my marketing and branding team, you can launch your book like a Rock Star!

Don't forget this book is really about, **"How to Turn Your Message, Cause, Expertise, or Your Business Card into a Book** Just Like this!"

And yes, a business card turned into a book makes you an author, but it also establishes you as an expert. The act of you championing your cause or sharing your message and expertise on the pages of a book like this will make you an author. Your book will be on sale on Amazon, Barnes and Noble, and other leading retailers.

Why You Need a Book

Everyone who has something to share or teach that can benefit others needs to write a book. Be it a message, cause, or you simply sharing your expertise. Writing a book can be easy to do, and you can write anything that your heart desires that people will be interested in reading. A 30 - 90-page book like this one is the ultimate sales tool, business card, and platform to get your message out.

Traditional business cards are always thrown away and forgotten, so you need to take the next step, and go the extra mile in creating the ultimate business card: a book just like this.

You don't have to write a long book, as long as you have valuable information that gets your point across. Writing a book is a new way to market and promote yourself, what you know, what you have experienced in the past, and what you stand for or against. If you are a business professional, then you need to write a book. If you are a celebrity, then you need to write a book. Anyone who has something important to say or something that people would like to learn needs to write a book. It's as simple as that, and I can't stress that enough.

Reasons You Need a Book

There are many excellent reasons professionals such as doctors, lawyers, celebrities, and dentists should write a book. For those who are in the medical profession, the average consumer wants to learn about new medical breakthroughs and ways that they can live a healthier life. For attorneys, people want to learn how they can win court cases and how to file bankruptcy, lawsuits, etc. Celebrities, along with successful entrepreneurs, have raving fans, and they all want to know how you worked your way up to becoming a success! There are so many reasons you should write a book, and people **WILL** want to read what you have to say! You can become an awesome success story once you become an awesome author of your own book!

Your Message, Your Cause, Your Expertise, or The Business Card Turned Book is Right for You and Your Profession

Let me share an example. Let's say you need braces. You visit two orthodontists in the same professional complex. The first orthodontist gives you a consultation and his business card. The other orthodontist, after the consultation, hands you a book titled *Braces vs. Dental Implants. Get the facts. Know Which Procedure is Right for You.* With all else being equal, which orthodontist would you most likely schedule an appointment with? Which "business card" would you be more likely to look at again?

Being an author in your field immediately gives you credibility and authority. Others will see you as the expert that you are and having a book will help you stand out from your competition. Since books are vehicles to deliver information, books also give you a way to provide instant value to your potential customers, establishing trust.

By detailing your expertise (what you do and why you do it, and how it benefits the reader/prospect) in a book, you can win over prospects and turn them into customers and clients.

Below are just a few professions/businesses that would benefit from a Business Card turned into a Book:

Architects

Accountants

Acupuncturists

Acting Coaches

Addiction Therapists

Chefs

Chiropractors

Coaches

Consultants

CPAs

Dance Instructors

Dentists

Dieticians

Deejays

Dog Trainers

Electricians

Event Planners

General Contractors

Hair Stylists

Home Improvement Specialists

House Painters

Landscapers

Massage Therapists

Mechanics

Mental Health Counselors

Occupational Therapists

Orthodontists

Personal Trainers

Gyms

Physical Therapists

Physicians

Plumbers

Pool Specialists

Rappers

Realtors

Restaurants

Roofers

Speakers

Tax Preparers

Tutors

Vets

Website Designers

Wedding Planners

And the list goes on . . . and on . . . and on . . .

Your Clients and Prospects are Better Educated About Your Business with a Book Like this

All you do is compile the basic "FAQs" (Frequently Asked Questions) and "SAQs" (Should Ask Questions) about your business, expertise, message, or cause. Answer them, put them in order of importance and group them and that will get your message across and educate your prospect. It will save you a lot of time delivering your usual introductory information, and it is your automated sales rep who never sleeps and who always nails the presentation 100% of the time. You even get to sell without being salesy! Your book becomes a vehicle to educate your prospects about your business, products and services, systems, and message about you.

You are actually magnifying recognition for your personal brand and increasing sales without salespeople. A book allows you to have a one-on-one with many people at the same time. When a prospect or client is reading your book, they are focused on you. You will be getting your message across quickly, thoroughly, and easily.

A book is an awesome networking tool. It helps you interact with all the people you want, delivering exactly what you want to say, without taking a lot of time.

You Will Achieve Better Results from Your Advertising

Use it to promote a webinar, teleseminar, or any presentation. Having made your prospects simply AWARE that you have a book heightens that awareness.

You can talk about the book or show the book in your advertising as a credibility booster and get higher responses.

Ads Capture Attention for Seconds . . . A Book Will Hold the Attention of Your Prospects Longer

Books Have Longevity and Viral Power – Since They Are Not Thrown Away

Books don't get lost in a drawer like a business card does. Books rest on shelves, desks, and countertops, in bathrooms, inside backpacks; and they are stored on e-reading devices. Books do not get tossed into the trash like sales letters or postcards. People just don't throw away books. They might get packed away. They might get donated or given away, but they are very rarely, if ever, trashed. I recall when moving, placing some books in the trash and then a few minutes later, taking them out! I just couldn't throw them away. Ever go to a flea market or auction and see a box of books? What is that natural instinct? To go through them. It is so exciting because you never know what magic or wisdom you may come across. Is there a better vehicle to deliver your message that is so widely valued and not disposed of within minutes? I don't think so.

We at W. Clark Distribution Media and Publishing Will Eliminate the Common Excuses for not Getting Your Book Completed!

Such as:

- I want to . . . but I'll eventually get around to it one of these days
- I don't have time
- I don't know how
- I'm not a writer
- I don't know what to write about

If you are still thinking there is no way you can write a book, remember that it doesn't have to be long. Simply brainstorm topics by thinking of questions you are asked most frequently. From that list you can create a book.

And you don't have to give away all of your knowledge in one book. Just give away one very specific nugget, filled with value that your potential clients would appreciate and thank you for.

Is Writing a Book for You?
The Answer to that is Yes, if:

- *you* want to speak at events or be interviewed on podcasts or talk shows

- *you* consider your business to be "missional"

- there are frequently asked questions that you have to answer for each new client

- *you* want to record lessons you learned

- *you* want to communicate principles you wish to pass on to others

- *you* have content that you can repurpose (republish) (blogs, articles, interviews, e-books, reports, etc.)

- *you* are running for any kind of public office

- *and more . . .*

Leveraging Your Book

Having your expertise, message, cause, or business card turned into a book gets even better! It can be used as leverage for greater opportunities. For some it might be speaking engagements, for others it might be product sales, and for you it might be getting more clients. If you are running for Governor, Senator, or President, it can be used as a fundraising tool and getting your message across to your potential base.

A book becomes another resource in your marketing funnel to lead them to your back-end offer. This means that you need to offer your readers, on top of great content and readability, a clear and direct call to action within your book. Even if they don't ever read a word, it needs to be clear to the person who is aware of your book what they need to do next.

Give it Away on Your Website as a Lead-generating Offer

Offer your book as a giveaway. In exchange you can collect names, e-mail addresses, and phone numbers, then move them directly to your follow-up campaign or onto an order page. Be sure to have your website, or any reference to a free report, webinar, etc., sprinkled throughout your booklet.

Depending on your offer, you can even ask for a small amount of money, e.g. $6.99 for processing and shipping and oftentimes gain a better and more qualified prospect. That is something that you would have to measure.

OTHER WAYS TO BUILD A BUSINESS WITH A BOOK

A Book Just like This can be used to get you high paid speaking gigs.

Who loves speakers?

- Non-profit groups
- Meeting Planners
- Religious Organizations
- Government and State Institutions
- Talk Show and Television Hosts
- And many, many more!

Create a Buzz in Your Industry so People Will Take Notice of You

If you want people in your industry to recognize your name, then you need to write, publish, and promote your book!

Send an Industry-Wide Message When You Write a Book

Do you consider yourself to be a Subject Matter Expert (SME) or guru in the industry you work in? Are you a doctor, lawyer, marketer, or other professional that has something to say to everyone who works in the same industry?

People are always seeking out more knowledge so they can improve their:

➢ Lives

➢ Health

➢ Careers

➢ Family

➢ Finances

If people believe you have something valuable in your book, they're going to buy your book and read it! They're also going to spread the word to as many people as they know!

Become a Subject Matter Expert (SME) In Your Profession!

To become a widely known SME, or to communicate to a large number of people, you need to become an author. This is the only way people will listen to what you have to say and believe that you are an SME in your profession or industry. Do you have knowledge about the:

- ✓ Health and Medical Industry?
- ✓ Fashion Industry?
- ✓ Legal Industry?
- ✓ Retail Industry?
- ✓ Celebrity Living?
- ✓ Cannabis Industry?
- ✓ Bitcoin Industry?
- ✓ Or Anything Else from the Endless List of Topics to Choose from?

If you are a wealth of information in any industry or profession, then you need to write a book! That is the *only way* you will be able to share secrets, tips, and advice with millions of people worldwide!

Use A Book Just Like This as an Additional Revenue Stream

A book can become an income stream. Thousands of companies buy books in bulk every year to use as premiums, gifts, employee training, marketing tools, etc. So, keep that in mind when putting your book together and do so accordingly.

Remember: What this book is really about is, "How To Turn your Message, Cause, Expertise, or your Business Card into a Book Just like this!"

What Type of Book Should You Write?

List Book

A *List Book* is an easy book to create and depending on the topic, can be extremely valuable to your audience. A *List Book* is simply that: a book that lists information. Why lists? Because they make it easy to brainstorm, organize, and write quickly and lists are easy to read. People love to read lists. And a good example of a List Book is: A general contractor creating a book that lists the repairs he specializes in, or "The 8 Ways a Leak Can Damage Your Home."

FAQ/SAQ Books (Frequently Asked Questions/Should Ask Questions)

A plastic surgeon could write a *SAQ* Book on the types of questions a patient should ask before getting liposuction. A literary agent could write a FAQ Book on how to acquire a major publisher, or the roles of a literary agent.

How-To Books

One of the biggest benefits of writing a How-To Book, in addition to it being extremely valuable, is that in many cases the bulk of the book can be pictures, not words.

What do you know that others don't? You'd be surprised at how many things you know that others would love to learn. Business "How-To" books are usually top sellers. Our team will show you how easily this is done.

Turning Your Business Card Into a Book

One of my editors, Alanna, commented on this manuscript. She said, *"Wahida, I see how you can Turn Your Message, Cause, or Expertise into a Book, but your Business Card? You've gone too far!"*

I thank her for that question because if she is a skeptic or just can't fathom how to do such a thing, that means there may be more of you skeptics out there!

So, let me give you an example. I went to my junk drawer and pulled out a random business card. (You know, that junk drawer where you toss all of the cards, loose change, pens, candy, etc., in.) Case in point, that's *exactly* why you need to turn your Business Card into a Book, so your card *won't* get tossed in a drawer somewhere and forgotten! You can't get new business that way.

I pulled a random card that said:

Onyx

Dyson Dinsmore, CCIM

Senior Property Manager

Now, for us business folks, our job is to get new clients and spread the word about what we do to get more clients. It's not rocket science . . . If we have no clients, we have no business. Pure and simple. So, when I looked at this card, I asked:

1. ONYX. What does that mean?

2. What kind of business is ONYX?

3. What exactly does Mr. Dinsmore do?

4. What does CCIM stand for?

5. Senior Property Manager. What are the responsibilities of a Senior Property Manager?

6. Manage what? Hotels, Bars, Apartments, Nursing Homes—what?

7. Whatever you manage, why is that your specialty?

8. Why do I need a property manager? Especially

you?

9. What makes your Property Management Company different from the one down the street?

10. How would you enhance my property?

11. How would you make my life easier/better?

I hope you get the picture. All Mr. Dinsmore has to do now is add another 10–15 questions about what he does, how he does it, why I need him, fill in the answers, and voilà! He has a book just like this one!

Also, another method I learned, you can place a Quick Response Code (QR Code) on a flyer or newsletter or actual business card that, when scanned, will lead directly to your book on Amazon, Barnes & Noble, or iBooks stores. I know it sounds boring or even difficult, but it is effective. It works.

Any book that you decide to write, we can help you with. Just shoot me an email at booking@wahidathecoach.com

Looking forward to partnering with you,
Wahida Clark

BONUS SECTION

How About My Book Title? How Do I Come Up with One?

This to me is one of the most exciting parts about writing! Coming up with the title. And yet for some, one of the most stressful parts. Some authors begin writing their book already knowing their title. Sometimes the title doesn't hit you until after you've written your book. Sometimes a sentence will stand out or scream at you. And that's your title. But when the right title hits you, you'll know it because it's magical.

Does the Book Cover Design Really Matter?

Absolutely! Your cover design can make or break your book. Some authors even test their designs. Meaning they post two to three designs and see which one gets the most views or positive comments. Yes, it is that serious. So, word of caution: do not cut corners when it comes to your cover or interior design. Remember: You get what you pay for. If you pay $75 for a book cover, it most likely is going to look like a $75 book cover. A good cover design *starts* around $350 and up.

You don't want to take a chance at choosing a book cover design that doesn't attract anyone that you're targeting. By testing out a few covers, you will soon find which one draws the most readers and traffic to your site to buy your book. And you want your book to look both fabulous and professional. You don't want to send Oprah a book that looks as if your cover and or interior (a double no-no) was designed right there on your smart phone. Be sure to request my Book Cover Check List.

I Don't Know the First Thing about Editing or Interior Book Design. Now What?

The majority of people who write their own book doesn't know anything about editing or book design. There are plenty of freelance editors and graphic designers that you can choose from online. You may want to first start out by looking into referrals or recommendations before you hire a freelancer from one of the freelance websites. You can also find good editors and designers on sites such as Freelancer and Upwork. But again *remember*, you get what you pay for. If you pay someone pennies on the dollar, then chances are, your graphic designer or editor will not produce the results you are expecting. A very good graphic designer for a cover grosses anywhere from $350 - $1,000. It all depends on how intricate, professional, and glamorous you want your cover to be.

Editing usually starts at around $3 - $4 per page and some start even higher. Interior Book Design can start around $150 depending on the pages of the book.

So, you need to do your research before you hire someone that you don't know online, especially if you have a limited budget! Be diligent, get references, and look at samples before hiring an online freelancer to perform your editing or interior layout for your book. And here's a TIP: Your book is a reflection of you. Don't hold back when it comes to adding your personality.

Why Do I Need a Website to Promote My Book?

Technology is always evolving and changing, so you will need to stay on top of the new ways to promote your book. The Internet and Social Media are at the top of the list when it comes to the best ways to promote your book and placing it in front of millions of people who are interested in the topic you are writing about.

This is the Internet and Social Media age. If Mrs. Marbles the Cat has a website, shouldn't you have one to promote your business, yourself, or your product? A book and a website go hand in hand. Your website is also your store to sell your books, services, and products. You will want to find a web designer that has experience in creating websites for authors so you can get the best chance at selling your book online.

However, if you only want to sell minimal copies of your book without a website, you can simply use Amazon, iBooks, and Barnes and Noble to send the traffic. You can also use funnel sites like Click Funnels or Book Funnels as well as YouTube, Roku, Fire TV, and more!

Pass your Message, Cause, Expertise, or Business Card turned into a Book to:

- editors of newspapers, blogs, and magazines to get interviews or a request to write articles
- book reviewers
- radio shows and podcast hosts for interviews
- promoters that host events and get speaking gigs
- clients as gifts
- list owners to get a teleseminar or webinar gig
- librarians and institutions
- associations and trade group leaders
- sell your coaching/consulting
- powerful or famous people you want to meet
- prospects who respond to an advertisement

Pass your book out at:

- places where your prospects might run into it
- business conferences
- business meetings
- speaking events where you are not selling

Make it available as:

- a bonus with a product or with your services
- a Kindle Book to get viral traction
- a free book offer on Social Media to your targeted prospects
- a requirement for new clients to read
- a reward for sticking around for a presentation
- a thank you gift to clients
- a promo tool when you do interviews for all types of media

Last but not least, and my favorite *give it away* to secure appointments and generate referrals or leads

"Just by showing up, you will get a gift valued at $9.95!" Gifting your book will create client loyalty and you can double your client retention.

Also, use the book to generate quality referrals, especially since over 70% of new clients come from referrals. Give it away to clients and ask them to pass it along to their family, friends, and colleagues. The book will guarantee that your message is delivered exactly the way you want it.

What if I want to Write Fiction, a Memoir, My Life Story, or a Children's Book?

That's not a problem. Again, I am a 4-time *New York Times* Best-Selling Author, with a winning team of experts, editors, writers, branding coaches, marketers and more. So, connecting you with the Write (pun intended) team who wants to see you win is a bonus. If you win, we win! That is the easy part.

Writing a fictional book is not easy. I don't care what anyone else says. Personally, I've written 15 or more books that are published and in print . . . writing a book is hard work and it takes discipline. I remember writing on deadline, and we had our first beautiful, spring day in

New Jersey. The springtime breeze was blowing through my window. I heard children playing and laughing, car horns honking, and music thumping through the car speakers. This was in 2008. But I was stuck inside writing while everyone else was out there enjoying the beginning of spring. Or you could be on a writing deadline while the entire family is headed out to the movies. You could be on deadline and it's 1:30 in the morning. While everyone is in a deep comatose sleep, you wish you were too, but instead you are up writing. That can be hard. Writing fiction, memoirs, and biographies is HARD WORK.

But . . . I Don't Know What to Write or How to Even Get Started. What Do I Do?

That's simple, and this is where we come in. If you are an entrepreneur or a celebrity, you first have to decide if you are going to do a List Book, How-To, or a FAQ/SAQ Book. If you are writing your List Book, start making your list. If you are writing the FAQ/SAQ Book, then you should jot down at least 10 questions that you are asked the most and 10 questions that you want your potential clients to ask. Then we will take it from there. Doing that simple task will allow our professional editorial staff to develop your book with you. If you want to write a tell-all, memoir, fiction, or TV script, email us at editor@wclarkdistribution.com. I will set up a phone conference with you and give you details about my book coaching programs.

It's Easy to Get Started!

Now that you are ready to write a book, it's easy to get started! All you need to do is contact us at W. Clark Distribution, Media and Publishing Company and we'll walk you through the process. We guarantee it'll be painless, and you will be able to make your own decisions on what you want your book to have in it. We will help you take your business card, message, or cause and turn it into an amazing booklet that you can use as a lead generator or promotional tool. You don't have any reason to not write a book!

The following is an example of what you can include in your book. I've inserted my Book Writing and Coaching Programs, as well as details for my Book Distribution Programs for the author or indie publisher. I'm sure that you already have material that you can insert in your book as well. However, this information is in real time and can be used NOW!

ON BOOK DISTRIBUTION

Nothing moves without distribution. Distribution, according to *Webster's Dictionary*, means: "to divide among many; spread or hand out."

So, if you are selling a product, book, CD, wig, etc., the wider and deeper your distribution platform, the more movement you have, the more revenue you create—and the more money you make.

And focused *Book Distribution* takes your book or books and makes them available to as many readers as possible in every way possible and gives it to them in the exact format they would like to read it.

So, you've written your book, and now, you are ready to sell it! It's mind-boggling to me why you go through all of that hard work of writing a book . . . to only sell it one way. Why leave all of that money on the table?

My ideal client writes to generate residual income from their books. The *W. Clark Distribution* platform was devised with that ideal client in mind. The authors who would benefit the most from my program are:

- You have written a book/s but only offer it to readers on Kindle

- You currently don't sell or market paperback versions of your book

- You are not in bookstores

- The audiobook, hardcover, libraries, Nook, Apple Book, large print consumers are simply out of luck because your book/s is not available on those platforms.

Distribution is EVERYTHING! We as authors hustle and grind, pulling countless all-nighters to get a book finished, so why not position ourselves to reap the maximum reward? Therefore, I MUST REPEAT!!! Why sell your book only on Amazon? Why sell your book only as an e-book? Why not sell paperbacks? Why not large print? Why not hardbacks? Why not on Kobo? Why not on Nook? Why not in the libraries? Audio books? *Why limit and block your book sales?*

In the *W. Clark Distribution* closed Facebook Group, this is where authors and small publishers can come, learn, and build your distribution platform. Do you need me in order for you to learn how to build your distribution platform? Yes and No! Do you need to use my Distribution Company to set up distribution for your titles? Yes and No! Here is the link to sign up for distribution with the world's largest book wholesalers, *Ingram Spark Pro*, https://ui.awin.com/publisher-signup/us/step1 (please note that I am one of their affiliates, and I do get compensation). Go Ahead! It's

FREE!
http://www.awin1.com/awclick.php?mid=4032&id=559
809 Click Now!

So, not everyone needs me. But I do say YES! to the authors who e-mail me and say, "Wahida, I understand that publishing is a business, and books are not written to be sold on just one platform. I also understand that in order to sell books, I have to invest in the marketing and distribution (meaning time and money) of my book/s." I am now available to work with you as your personal coach.

I am also saying YES! to those authors who constantly e-mail me and ask how to launch and distribute their book/s. This is YOUR opportunity to work with me. This program is for YOU, the author who wants to work with a 4x (Four-Time New York Times Best-Selling Author) NYT Best Seller of 3 Best-Selling series and Publisher of over 70 novels, including 10 Series, Celebrity Ghostwriter, and Business Book Coach.

At *W. Clark Distribution*, we take advantage and embrace current Print-on-Demand (POD) technology. We love it because it turns authors into publishers without having to warehouse inventory, take chances on projected sales, and authors don't have to invest heavily on packing supplies and shipping of boxes and endless trips to the post office while they waste time standing in line.

But the key in utilizing the POD technology is you must have the right wholesale partners and have your book pricing right to get in bookstores and libraries.

Now, you don't have to go with learning all about book distribution, formatting, and price points alone. The *W. Clark Distribution Beta Program* shows authors and small publishers **HOW TO SELL MORE BOOKS** by positioning their title in every possible format, meaning, e-book, paperback, hardback, large print, and audio by simply utilizing the ***W. Clark All-Formats and Book Publishing and Marketing Checklist* . . .** all while having *Wahida Clark*, a four-time NYT Winner, as YOUR personal coach! It doesn't get any better than that! Go at it alone . . . or Team Up with Wahida!

If you make the investment in time and consistency (do the work), then in 90 days, your title will be in every format, and you are at least 3X'ing (tripling) your book sales. And you get to work with a four-time New York Times Best-Selling Author during this Beta Launch . . . Team up with an official and established book brand and platform. You won't find a better accountability team!

USE THE CHECKLIST! IT WORKS!!

Let's make it happen!

So, there you have it! I've shared with you, how to write, what to write, and priceless info on book distribution. All you have to do now is apply it. For those of you who feel that you may need a little more hand holding or one-on-one support here are our packages:

SAMPLE OF COACHING PACKAGES

"Twenty Minute "What to do Next" Coaching Package

This package is for you if:

1. You are working on your book project and feeling STUCK

2. You are procrastinating or worrying about the structure of your book, what to do next or finding the right audience to target

3. You have been dying to work with four-time *New York Times* Best Seller and Publisher, Wahida Clark to give you guidance on your Book Project

What you Get: a twenty (20) minute One-on-One Strategy and Coaching Call. All is required of you is to show up on the Coaching Call with your questions, comments, or ideas ready! Not only will Wahida provide you with solutions to getting your book written, she will also put you on the road to being published, promoted, and/or distributed.

*If during the course of your Coaching Call you elect to use our services and want Wahida to put you on the Fast-Track, the fee will then be credited to your brand-new package.

"Turn that Idea or Scene in your Head into a Movie Script or Book" Consulting Package

This package is for you if:

1. You have a scene that plays in your head and you're not sure why or where it comes from. But now you want to know what to do with it. Is it a movie? A book? An episode to a TV pilot? A Broadway Play? A signature speech?

For Your Investment you will receive a 30-minute one-on-one consultation and strategy session with four-time *New York Times* (NYT) Best-seller Wahida Clark. Together you will take that scene or idea in your head and create an outline. Or, if you already know what you want to do with your project, but you need Wahida's assistance in its execution, that can be decided as well.

The investment will be credited if you hire her to write a book, outline, script, episode, etc.

"Turn that Idea, Hobby, Expertise, or Training into a Book Now!" Consulting Package

This package is for you if:

1. You have an idea, or you have been collecting data, writing down notes in hopes of getting it all organized into a book. But there's one problem. . . You're not quite sure how to organize and structure it.

Great News! You can now gain access to your *One-on-One Gain Clarity and Strategy Session* with a four-time *NYT* Best Seller and Writing and Publishing Coach. This is your time to share your goals about your idea, hobby, or training with Wahida. During this session, you can explain what you are trying to achieve—your end goal/your vision/and your project details. Your *personalized* Gain Clarity and Strategy Session.

You will use this 40-minute period to gain clarity and outline a strategy that Wahida can put into an itemized Get-It-Done Checklist for you.

After you receive your checklist, you will be able to put your book together, but if you don't want to do it alone, our *"How to Get It Written Program and Publisher's Program"* for nonfiction authors may be an option for you. It includes cover design, professional copyedits by editors who edit for major publishing houses, interior layout, design and book distribution. Your first written book can be the start of Your Own Publishing Empire. And remember, a book is designed to bring in *recurring revenue month after month!*

Nonfiction Package Investment

*email us for details

Memoirs, Biographies, etc., Package Investment

*email us for details

Fiction

*email us for details

"Make Your Book Pop" Consulting Package

This package is for you if:

1. You have a book but are unsure how to launch it ... Correctly and Like a Pro!

2. You want feedback on your cover and overall

book presentation

3. You want feedback on your manuscript (from a four-time NYT Best-selling author)

4. You want to establish your books' brand and/or get brand clarity

The **"Make Your Book Pop"** Consulting Package includes but is not limited to:

1. Critique and overview

2. Critique of book cover and appearance (Will it stand tall against the other titles on the shelf?)

3. A manuscript read and critique (everyone doesn't request this)

4. Outline Your Blueprint for Your Book Movement to be Launched and Establish Your Brand

5. Newsletter and Facebook Group Set-up and Launch

*Any critique or feedback can be given verbally or written

"You Say You Want to Dominate" Consulting Package

This package is for you if:

1. You have a book but are unsure how to launch it . . . **Correctly and Like a Pro!**

2. You want feedback on your cover and overall book presentation

3. You want feedback on your manuscript (from a **four-time NYT Best-selling** author)

4. You want to **Establish** your **Books' Brand** and/or **Get Brand Clarity**

5. You don't have the time to take it to this level on your own and would rather focus on promoting or running your **Book Business**

The **"You Say You Want to Dominate" Consulting Package** includes but is not limited to:

1. Critique and Overview

2. Critique of Book Cover and Appearance (Will it stand tall against the other titles on the shelf?)

3. A Manuscript Read and Critique (everyone doesn't request this)

4. Outline Your Blueprint for Your Book

Movement to be Launched and Establish Your Brand

5. Newsletter and Facebook Group Set-up and Launch

6. New Book, e-book, Hardcover and Audiobook Cover Design

7. Interior Layout files for Paperback, e-book, Hardcover

8. Manuscript Edit

9. Audiobook Narrator

10. Facebook, Instagram, and Twitter Banners

11. Logo Design

12. Book Launch Campaign Set-up (90 days before Release date)

*Publicist 1 - 3 Months (additional)

"Launch Like a Rock Star or Best-Selling Author" Consulting Package

Not everyone thinks they are a Rock or Rap Star. But if you do, then the **"Launch Like a Rock Star or Best-Selling Author" Consulting Package has your name on it!!! You are undoubtedly in it to win it and want to show your competition NO MERCY!**

You get everything that's in the **"You Say You Want to Dominate" Consulting Package** but is not limited to:

1. Critique and Overview

2. Critique of Book Cover and Appearance (Will it stand tall against the other titles on the shelf?)

3. A Manuscript Read and Critique (everyone doesn't request this)

4. Outline Your Blueprint for Your Book Movement to be Launched and Establish Your Brand

5. Newsletter and Facebook Group Set-up and Launch

6. New Book, e-book, Hardcover and Audiobook Cover Design

7. Interior Layout files for Paperback, e-book, Hardcover

8. Manuscript Edit

9. Audiobook Narrator

10. Facebook, Instagram, and Twitter Banners

11. Logo Design

12. Book Launch Campaign Set-up (90 days before Launch date)

13. Book Publicist for 3 months (included)

14. Video Sales Letter Package

15. Podcast Channel Package

16. YouTube Channel Package

17. Pitch to Television Network Basic Package

18. Book Launch Campaign Set-up and Launch

*Speaking Engagement Publicist 1 - 3 months *optional*

Once again I've given you all of the major tools to write, publish, and sell. Even if you don't hire our services, this is the blueprint of what and how to publish, launch and continue your quest for growth and knowledge.

CONCLUSION

I know that I overdelivered to you, my methods of How to turn your Message, Cause, Expertise, and Business Card into a Book. And remember, everyone that is someone has a book. It doesn't have to be 375 pages. It doesn't have to be long and drawn out. In today's swift social media climate, we all want our information uncut, fast delivered on channel WIFM. What's in it for me. Give us want we want, now, no holds barred, no blowing smoke.

I've also given you in this little book the powerful keys of getting your book written/finished and published! I've wiped away all of the excuses!

My mission should you choose to accept, is to make sure that in 45 days or less, you seize this moment to get that 1st draft of the outline or book you've been struggling to write, finish or get out of your head, so that the weight of accomplishment is off your shoulders, another big win is under your belt, and use your book to spread your message, establish yourself as the expert or get more speaking engagements or clients.

Wahida Clark

ABOUT THE AUTHOR

Wahida Clark is also known as the Official Queen of Street Literature. She is a Celebrity Book Writing Coach, Celebrity Ghostwriter and author of 15 titles, including 4 New York Times Best-Sellers. She is the Business Development Officer of W. Clark Book Distribution and is a lover of anything books . . . Writing , Publishing and Promoting.